I0116646

The

Manifesto

Of

The African Peoples

Independence Party

ISBN 978-1-906914-78-3

Ben Nnolim Books,
7 Sandway Path,
St Mary Cray,
Orpington, Kent
BR5 3TS, UK
Email: benedictnnolim@aol.com

Dedication

This Manifesto is dedicated to all peoples of Sub-Saharan Africa

Table of Contents

PREAMBLE:
THE NEED FOR A NEW, TRULY, AFRICAN PARTY

The Colonial Angle

African countries, south of the Sahara, are, currently, suffering from the deliberate and oppressive arrangements of the European colonial powers in which diverse African tribes were corralled together for administrative and economic convenience. Each of these contraptions, misnamed countries, was given a name, usually suggested at the drinking club or by the wife of one of the colonialists, and the peoples of this artificial arrangement were told that this name was the name of their new country. They were taught the European language of their colonisers and when they agitated for it, were given "independence".

The result is that every one of most African countries, south of the Sahara, today can be likened to a country formed from merging Italy, France, Spain, Switzerland, Belgium, Holland, the United Kingdom, Portugal, Denmark, Norway, Finland, Poland, Hungary, etc, as one country, taught Chinese as their national language and advised to live in peace and national unity.

To put it another way, it is like getting four, five or more brothers, born of the same mother, to live in one house with their wives, children and their in-laws and telling them that they are all brothers and sisters who are expected to live in peace and unity with each other.

Meanwhile, they, the Europeans, did the opposite and natural thing. They got their tribes to live as separate countries. When they get together to form the European or any union, they do so as independent cohesive countries, even though they, still, do not, often, agree.

They did not even get to this stage amicably. They fought and killed each other for hundreds of years until their proper relationships and alliances could be definitely established. In some places such as Belgium and the United Kingdom, the intertribal war has not ended and is still being fought even if in different ways.

It is worthy of note that, at the time the European tribes were fighting among themselves, African tribes were also doing a similar thing. There were two major differences, however. One was that having been conquered by the Romans, Greeks and other ancient civilisations, Europeans had acquired more experience of war and its intrigues than Africa so that when they came to Africa, Africans had no chance, not with bows and arrows and unwritten languages against guns, cannons, warships and tested, written, military and colonising strategies.

Although there were, and still are, certainly, cultural and societal differences among African tribes, south of the Sahara, these differences are, surprisingly, minor. In fact the major differences are those introduced, not by the variety of their indigenous languages, culture and norms, but by the different European languages and cultures they have been forced and taught to speak or learn.

Secondly, Europeans were driven to Africa by scarcity of resources in their harsh environments and their need to get the upper hand against their European competitors. Thus while they fought and killed each other to establish their national identities, they stopped Africa south of the Sahara, from doing a similar thing. While they denigrated similar African identity wars as tribal wars among primitive tribes, they eulogised theirs as national wars of liberation, succession, freedom or whatever noble sounding objectives they could use to sanitise the carnage and brutality of their wars.

It needs to be pointed out that all the death and destruction of all African tribal wars since time began and prior to colonisation, put together, cannot equal the death, rape and physical destruction of the smallest European war.

All the African countries south of the Sahara are victims. Consisting of, in some countries, up to 250 tribes with languages and culture as varied as those between Dakar and Pretoria, they were formed by either, the British, the French, the Belgians, the Germans or the Portuguese. A lot has been written and said, especially, during the independence campaign days, about colonial rule in African countries south of the Sahara. There have been civil wars in the Congo, in Nigeria, in Angola, in Rwanda, in Sierra Leone, in Liberia, in Ivory Coast, in Niger, in Chad, in Sudan to name but the most widely reported wars in Africa south of the Sahara.

What is on ground, today, however, is that there is continuous conflict and instability in these countries. In each and every one of these countries, there are always those tribes that first came in contact with Europeans who, thus, claim, if not superiority over the other tribes on this premise, at least the entitlement to a lion's share in the management of the new country's affairs. There are reluctant tribes who have to be persuaded, cajoled or bribed to stay in the union. There are tribes that are forced to belong to the union because they are powerless to do otherwise. And there are tribes that belong because they really have no choice either way.

In spite of all the exhortations and efforts by Christianity and Islam and of the sanctimonious lectures from Europe, USA and the United Nations urging national unity, social, political and economic policies in these countries are, intrinsically, incapable of dealing with their predicaments. These countries are divided countries in which every tribe and everybody is suspicious of every other tribe and person. Even the rulers, chiefs, presidents, governors, senators, legislators, university lecturers, bank managers, traders, business men and women in these countries have very little faith in their country and prefer to keep their financial assets outside the country. There can be little or no progress, no justice or self fulfilment in such a country or situation.

The African Angle

Archaeological and anthropological evidence confirm that human existence and civilization originated in eastern Africa. According to modern scholarship, the rest of the human race, including Asian and European peoples, were migrants from eastern Africa who migrated north west and north eastwards to the middle east from where the migration split into two, one going further east and the other westwards. This happened at the time the earth was one land mass before it separated into the continents of today as we know them. Genetic evidence suggests that the African has the most complete genes of all existing human beings and that is why they are able to transform into other races and at the same time survive as the original race.

But what does history tell us about Africans?

Historical evidence illustrates very clearly and forcefully that Africans have always been slaves to every civilisation, starting from the most ancient known civilisation to the present Western civilisation.

Africans have, also, been the butt of jokes, derisions and unthinkable cruelties from the European and Middle Eastern races, practices which found cruel expression in the slave trade on the east and west coasts of Africa and in the Americas.

Even religious books such as the Bible and epic poems such as Homer's Iliad and the Odyssey had verses which were interpreted, correctly or incorrectly, to justify the racial inferiority, and hence the maltreatment, of black peoples

In the nineteen sixties when Africans, south of the Sahara, were getting "independence", it was popular among African politicians to convince themselves and their followers that the ancient Egyptians, who built the pyramids and the Sphinx, were black Africans. When that hypothesis was placed in doubt by critical scholarship, they ran to Nubia. When that refuge seemed entirely

10

trivial, they ran to the empires of Ghana, Melle and Songhai.

Zimbabwe has been a difficult nut to crack although some speculation, based on the book by Rider Haggard, *King Solomon's Mines*, might suggest that Zimbabwe may have been built by King Solomon or during his reign.

As African politicians gave up this search for credible identity, based on European standards, in their desperate preoccupation with holding on to power, it fell to African academics, funded and supervised by European and American Universities, to search for some evidence that Africans, like everybody else, had a civilization. Thus, the Zimbabwe myth, the Ashanti culture, the Ghana, Melle, Songhai and Benin empires, the Nok culture, Ife bronze and several ancient African societies kept turning up in one PhD thesis after another.

When this search for the past became tiring and boring and the computer revolution came, Africans were still preoccupied with seeking the "golden fleece" in Europe and America while those they left behind fought and killed themselves over what the colonialists left at independence.

Jason and the Argonauts sought the Golden Fleece because it was reputed to be the solution to the problem they had in their native land. When Africans sought their "golden fleece" it was not for the purpose of solving the problems of their homeland but for the opportunity to lord it over their people as the colonialists did.

The end result is that while, from the 14th to the early 19th centuries, Africans were forcibly enslaved and carried away to the Americas or forced to trek through deserts to the Middle East, Africans are, in the 20th and 21st centuries, drowning in the Mediterranean sea, smuggling themselves into Europe in articulated goods lorries as illegal immigrants and asylum seekers begging to be enslaved.

Their leaders are busy selling their natural resources and

transferring the proceeds to Europe, North and South America and to anywhere else but Africa while their people are starving without any credible physical, social, cultural, educational, health or any infrastructure or process conducive to, or commensurate with, the endowment of the region.

It has, fortunately, been recognised by generation after generation of Africans since their various "independences", that Africa needs a new and workable mindset with regard to its politics, its governments and it social organisation.

It is also a fact that quite a few have tried. But colonial brainwashing and intrigue die hard. Altruism has become rare, especially; among those whose recipe for survival or self worth is hatred, egocentricity, greed, conflict, contests and purposeless intrigue. Thus, even though the colonialists have gone, they still manage to manipulate Africa and Africans by their unity of purpose and exploitation of African tribal jealousies.

All the education given to young Africans seem to have been wasted on them as most miss the point of the education and see it only as a means of appearing to be better than their contemporaries and for feathering their own nests at the expense of everybody else including their own future and that of their children.

It is appropriate, therefore, that as we progress into the 21st century AD, another attempt be made, and continues to be made, until Africa recognises its place and duty to its citizens and to the comity of nations.

This attempt is the formation of a model political party to be emulated in all current African countries, south of the Sahara. The name may be different in different countries but the objective must be, first, to, truly, return Africa and the management of its affairs to its peoples and, secondly, and concomitantly, to begin to take seriously, the exploitation and management of its vast resources for the benefit of its peoples.

This model party I have chosen to name the African Peoples Independence Party. If it operates in Nigeria, it could be called the Nigerian African Peoples' Independence Peoples Party (NAPIP) or the African Independence Peoples' Party of Nigeria (AIPPN). In Ghana it would be called the Ghanaian African Independence Peoples Party (GAPIP) or the African Independence Peoples' Party of Ghana (AIPPG) and so on. Many things can be done with names, however.

For example, if the word "Peoples" is left out, the name of the model party could be the African Independence Party (AIP). If "African" is substituted for with the name of the different countries, it could be, in Kenya, the Kenya Independence Party (KIP) or the Independence Party of Kenya (IPK) or in Uganda, the Uganda Independence Party (UIP) or the Independence Party of Uganda (IPU), etc. The word "Africa" or the name of the country could be omitted entirely to have the name of the party as the Peoples' Independence Party (PIP). The name of the party could, however, be something entirely different and not containing one word in the name African Peoples Independence Party provided its aims and objectives are those of this party.

THE MANIFESTO OF THE AFRICAN PEOPLES INDEPENDENCE PARTY (APIP)

Thus, the first objective of the African Peoples' Independence Party (APIP) in any African country, south of the Sahara, is to identify, by referendum, those tribes and peoples who wish to, willingly and freely, belong to the same country, under one set of accepted rule of law and practice.

As part of this objective, APIP notes that certain tribal groups are to be found dispersed among the presently neighbouring European established countries of West, Central, East and Southern Africa. For example, the Yorubas are found in Nigeria, Togo, Dahomey, Benin; the Hausas in Nigeria, Chad, Niger, Mali, Ghana, etc. The Tutsi are in Rwanda, Cameroons and Nigeria and so on.

A major foreign policy plank of the APIP would be to encourage the reunion of these tribes, presently scattered among the current Europe-synthesised countries, to form their own countries where their tribal language becomes their national language, as it was meant to be, and English, French, Portuguese, etc, become secondary and learned languages.

Once, or as, the association of similar, free and willing peoples becomes the basis of formation of countries in Africa, south of the Sahara, the second objective of the APIP is to release and nurture the creative and industrious energy of the peoples of these countries for the betterment and progress of their lives by the specific policies enumerated below.

1. ## The Constitution of the Genuine African Countries

    The constitution of any country should be the agreed and stated general principles which are expected, with minor changes from time to time, to guide political, social and juridical activities in the country and be valid at all times. It is different from the operational sets of laws which

15

implement these general principles of the constitution in time and place. Under APIP these laws will be made to comply with the constitutional provisions both in spirit and in fact.

The major cause of political upheaval in the majority of current African countries south of the Sahara is that they operate their constitutions as if they were laws for daily and every issue use. They do not pass the sufficient number and scope of operational laws which are based on the constitution.

Trying to use the constitution as an operational law exposes it, like all operational codes of law, to different interpretations and thus making disputes over interpretation causes for rancour between parties of different persuasions. When judges, with or without sympathies to one persuasion or the other, rule on such a constitutional issue, therefore, the chances are that the ruling becomes objectionable to the other party or parties and because there is no further remedy beyond the constitution, war or social disruption inevitably results.

The APIP will emphasise and enforce the distinction between the constitution, as a reference document, and other laws which implement the constitution in time and place. It will subject the ratification of every part of this constitution to a national referendum.

2. The Operational Codes of Law

All the existing law in the newly formed country will be revised to ensure compliance with the new constitution. Every such law must be associated with a time or period of validity to be determined by the legal experts and with options for the time and conditions of renewal, amendment or repeal.

3. Citizenship

    Citizenship shall be by parentage of either father or
    mother and by naturalisation. All marriages, births and
    deaths shall be associated with DNA record of the
    newlywed, the newly born and the newly dead. All
    visitors into the country must have their DNA taken and
    recorded while citizens would have their DNA record
    embedded in their passports

4. Levels of Government

    There shall be three levels of government, local, state and
    national. Local governments shall be demarcated on the
    basis of affinity of cultural/ethnic values and history and
    population of adult voters not less than one hundred
    thousand but not more than three hundred thousand.

    States shall, again, be demarcated on the basis of
    cultural/ethnic affinity and history and shall be established
    in such a way that though the states may not, necessarily,
    have the same number of local government areas. The
    population of states shall, preferably, not exceed three
    million adult voters

    There shall be only one national government.

5. Representation in Government

    Representation in government shall be by councillors in
    the local government, assembly men or women or
    legislators in the state assembly and senators in the
    national assembly. There shall not be more than one
    legislative assembly at any level of government.

    The chief executive of the local government shall be the
    local government chairman, that of the state, the governor
    and that of the national government, the president. There

17

shall be no legislators at the national level other than senators.

The basic unit of political representation shall be wards each of which shall consist, in homogenous communities, of a minimum of five hundred eligible voters. The only exception shall be in heterogeneous communities where ethnic minorities with less than 500 eligible voters shall be allowed to constitute a ward. Heterogeneity shall be based only on indigenous tribal or ethnic, not religious, educational, social or political, affinity.

The ward shall be the unit for elections to the local government assembly or council.

Constituencies shall be solely for the purpose of state and national elections and shall be made up of an equal number of wards to be determined by the appropriate electoral agency.

Each councillor in the local government shall represent not less than thirty thousand eligible voters.

Each state assembly man or woman shall represent not less than three hundred thousand eligible voters.

Each national senator shall represent not less than one million registered voters.

The APIP supports two options with regard to equality of representation in local government, state and the national legislature. The first option is the equality of votes of all elected representatives. This has the apparent advantage of assuring each citizen that all voting rights are equal. Its major disadvantage is that for local governments, states or countries with a lopsided ethnic majority/minority ratio, the ethnic minorities have, more or less, no vote as they would be always outvoted by the majority. This is, essentially, un-African. The second option considers that since the local governments and states may have lopsided ethnic majority/minority ratios, and thus may not have an equal number of councillors, state assembly men or women and senators because their numbers are based on population of eligible voters. This option feels that minority ethnic groups are better protected, not by giving them an equal number of representatives as the larger ethnic groups or subsuming their ethnic group within the surrounding or nearest larger ethnic group but by giving each group of ethnic representatives, in the local government, state or national legislature, veto powers on selected and agreed local, state or national issues. Such veto powers are to be valid only with unanimous support of the totality of the ethnic representatives in that legislature. Whichever option is chosen shall be determined by a referendum vis a vis the ethnic distribution in the areas in which the people have decided to belong to the same country.

6. Political Parties

Political parties are associations of people who share the same objectives, perspectives and conviction on the means of achieving those objectives. They help galvanise sections of the populace who share the same views and perspectives in order to get fair representation in the national discourse. Because there must be divergence of objectives, perspectives and methods in any modern democratic society, the APIP shall not limit the number of political parties.

Political parties shall not be required to have local, state or national spread but must be registered with the legitimate electoral commission

There shall, however, be three types of political parties namely, local government area parties, state parties and federal or national parties. Nothing in this precludes any of these from being an independent party.

Local Government Area Parties

Local government area parties can only, normally, field candidates in a local government election. Local government area parties cannot field candidates in a state or national election. For a local government area party to field candidates in a state election, it must have scored not less than forty percent of popular votes or won not less than forty percent of the seats in the local government council election in two previous consecutive local government elections.

Local government area parties shall not, normally, field candidates in a national election except in the first election in the first term of office of the African Peoples Independence party (APIP)

State Parties

State parties shall arise only from local government area parties which have won not less than forty percent of the popular vote or the number of seats in two previous consecutive local government elections.

State parties, normally, would field candidates in a state election. State parties cannot field candidates in a local government or national election. For a state party to field candidates in a national election, it must have scored not less than forty percent of popular votes or won not less than forty percent of the seats in the state house of assembly in two previous consecutive state government elections.

State parties shall not, normally, field candidates in a national election except in the first election in the first term of office of the African Peoples Independence party (APIP)

National Parties

National parties shall arise only from state parties which have won not less than forty percent of the popular vote or the number of seats in their state legislature in two previous consecutive state government elections.

There will be no need for state parties to have national spread if they meet the above criteria to contest a national election.

National parties cannot field candidates in a local government area or state elections.

For a national party to field candidates in a national election, it must have scored not less than twenty five percent of popular votes or seats in sixty five percent of the states in two previous national election. Otherwise it shall participate only in state elections..

The purpose of these regulations is to ensure that the democratic space is not monopolised by permanent national or state parties. Parties must survive as state or national parties depending on their continued acceptance by the electorate in these roles. Thus a party may be a national party today and a state or local government party tomorrow and vice versa.

If no party succeeds in qualifying to be a national party, state parties shall nominate senators to serve in a national government who will then elect a president. Such senators and president shall have only one term of two years with no opportunity to contest other and future national elections.

21

Registration of Parties

All initial party registrations shall be at the local government area level by any group of three or more persons who present a party constitution and evidence that each has been in gainful and steady employment in the past five years and duly paid their due taxes in those years.

They shall also present evidence of their financial assets and the sources and manner of acquisition of those assets, regardless of the magnitude or value of those assets. Any illegality in acquisition of those assets, as determined by a properly constituted court of, or by an existing, law, shall disqualify such persons from forming a political party

The designated electoral agency shall determine affordable fees which will not reduce eligibility for party registration to ability to pay but which may contribute to viable funding of a designated fraction of the particular electoral activity.

Membership of the Party

Membership of the party is open to all citizens of the country of sound mind, twenty one years of age and above, regardless of sex, tribe or religion.

The minimum educational qualification for membership shall be the first school leaving certificate.

The minimum educational qualification for holding any office in the local government area of the party shall be the secondary school certificate recognised as such in that country with at least five credit passes in two sittings while for the state or national offices of the party, the minimum educational qualification shall be the first degree (BA, BSc) or the equivalent qualifications in the teaching and other professions from an accredited institution for such certificates.

All prospective party officials shall have had not less than five years of gainful employment, with all appropriate taxes duly paid in those years.

Registration and Membership Fees

Membership and registration fees shall be determined by the appropriate party committee and as approved by the general convention of the party.

Officers of the Party

The officers of any political party, who must all be elected by the party convention, shall be as follows

a. Chairman of the Party
b. Executive committee to consist of one representative from each ward, constituency or senatorial zone depending on whether it is a local government, state or national party
c. Vice chairman, secretary, financial secretary, treasurer and publicity secretary for each of the national, state and local government executive committees
d. Chairman of the Arbitration Committee
e. Arbitration committee to consist of one representative from each ward, constituency or senatorial zone
f. depending on whether it is a local government, state or national party

These offices shall be filled by election according to the party's policy on elections and shall have the tenure, unless terminated by illness or other unforeseen circumstance, of not more than two years.

Each of the executive and arbitration committees is independent of each other and is responsible only to the national convention.

This independence does not imply or mean that they become tyrants and gods themselves. The independence is conferred on them to enable them discharge their duties without fear or favour in the interest of the country and that of the party.

The Annual Convention of the Party

The annual convention of the party shall be held annually in a location and venue to be selected at the previous convention and on rotation from local government to local government or state to state as the case may be.

The local government or state selected for an annual convention shall be responsible for nominating a venue for the convention in consultation with the local government affected.

The presiding officers in an annual convention shall be different from the above listed officers of the party who will be reporting their activities to the convention. They shall be members of the Convention Organising Committee made up of a chairman, secretary, publicity secretary, and a number of rapporteurs as deemed necessary for the convention proceedings itself and chairman, secretary, financial secretary and other members of specific activities such as transport, accommodation, publicity, etc, for the background organisation of the convention.

Their tenure shall begin one year ahead and end one year after the convention. Their remuneration and method of selection shall be as determined by the convention.

They shall, also, be responsible for producing the report of the proceedings of the convention which will then be material for the various executive committees to work with.

Other Officers and Committees of the Party

The party shall set up, from time to time and as required, a variety of consultancies and committees on politics, economy, religion, education, technology, and any other issues which the party may consider necessary to obtain expert advice and input. Only those consultancies and committees approved in an annual convention shall be funded by the party at the cost explicitly specified before the convention approval. The manner of staffing, remuneration and control of these consultancies and committees shall, also, be specified and approved by the annual convention

Disputes

All disputes within the party shall be shall be settled at the level at which they occur with no interference from any other party level. If a party dispute goes to court, such a party shall be suspended from participation in any electoral process until the court determines the dispute.

A certified and signed notice by all the contending parties that the dispute is settled shall be conveyed to the legally constituted electoral commission. Failure to settle the dispute, after six months, outside an election period or within two weeks in an election period, results in automatic suspension of membership of the party of all the disputing members.

Setting up a Party Branch

Party branches can be set up at ward or local government

levels for all parties. As soon as the necessary local government, state or national qualification required by the law on party registration is met, such a branch is considered to be set up in law provided it is registered with the electoral commission.

7. Collusion between Parties

The APIP shall outlaw collusion between parties across or within levels of the political landscape such as that between local government, state and national parties or between parties within the local government, state or nation. This is to give the electorate genuine and independent power to choose who shall represent them at any level.

8. Elections

Frequency

All elections shall be conducted at the times and frequency specified by the constitution. APIP believes that councillors should be elected every two years, state legislators every four years and national senators every six years. The president shall be elected every four years.

All the elected local government area, state and national legislators including the president can only be elected for two consecutive terms. He or she cannot be elected again after one or two terms of office.

The reason for this is to make sure that the democratic process is continually relevant to the wishes, and under the control, of the electorate rather than to an experienced cabal which masters and manipulates the electoral processes, have run out of ideas or energy and yet difficult to replace.

Eligibility to Vote

All citizens, twenty one years of age and above, except prisoners, those convicted of a criminal offence or offences and people certified to be of unsound mind, shall be eligible to vote.

To be eligible to vote in any election in any ward or constituency, such a citizen must have lived, worked and paid taxes in that ward or constituency for a minimum of two years or as shall be determined by the appropriate electoral agency, provided that the term determined is not less than two years.

Resident non-citizens of, and visitors to, the country, are not eligible to vote.

Responsibility to Vote

All citizens shall be required by law to cast their votes in any election. Every effort shall be made to facilitate voting by every citizen whether hospitalised or not and wherever they are after which it shall be a punishable offence not to cast one's vote in two consecutive elections. Abstention votes shall be allowed in all elections.

Quorum for a Valid Election

The quorum, for any election to be valid, shall, therefore, be forty percent of registered voters.

Winner of an Election

The winner of any election, for the posts of councillor, state legislator or senator, shall be that candidate who scores, in a free and fair election, the highest number of votes calculated in the following manner.

No matter the number candidates in an election, each voter shall be required to vote for any three preferred candidates as first choice, second choice, third choice only.

In counting the votes, the first choice candidate's vote shall count as five votes, the second choice candidate's vote shall count as three votes while the third choice candidate's vote shall count as one vote. All other candidate's votes shall count as zero votes.

When there is a tie, the candidate with the highest first choice votes wins the election.

For the posts of local government chairman, governor and president, respectively, the winner of the election is that candidate who scores, in a free and fair election, the highest number of votes calculated in manner of first, second and third choice votes. In addition, he or she has to get, at least, twenty five percent of votes in sixty five percent of all the wards, constituencies or states, respectively, calculated, also, in the manner of first, second and third choice votes.

The First Election in the First Term of the African Peoples Independence Party

Because local government area, state and national parties, as herein described, will not exist during the first term of office of the African Peoples Independence Party, all existing parties, including the African Peoples Independence Party, shall be, automatically, dissolved one year before the first election. All new parties will have to be registered as described above in a local government area.

Because there would not have been state and national parties in this first term, all parties which must be registered at the local government level, shall be entitled to contest all elections at the local government area, state and national levels in two respective consecutive elections after which the rules for local government, state and national parties will begin to apply in the third election.

Candidates for Election

A candidate for any election shall be of sound mind and not convicted of any criminal offence in any court of law. In addition, he or she must be not less than twenty one years of age and must have been in gainful and steady employment with all due taxes paid in the five years preceding the year in which he or she seeks to be elected.

He or she shall also present evidence of his or her financial assets and the sources and manner of acquisition of those assets, regardless of the magnitude or value of those assets. Any illegality in acquisition of those assets, as determined by a properly constituted court of, or by an existing, law, shall disqualify such persons from contesting the election

Such a candidate shall be accepted to contest the election either as an independent candidate or as a member of a duly registered party and duly nominated by his or her own party. In either case, the candidacy must be supported by one other person meeting the same eligibility requirements as the contestant.

A government, public service or private sector employee can stand for elected office but must take an unpaid two year sabbatical or leave of absence from his or her employment one year before contesting for the election. Such employees, if they lose the election, shall be entitled to resume their appointments at the expiration of the sabbatical.

The designated electoral agency shall determine affordable fees, for registration of candidates for an election, which will not reduce eligibility for election to ability to pay but which may contribute to viable funding of a designated fraction of the particular electoral activity.

Election Campaigns

Election campaigns shall be by only the candidates contesting the election and shall be by personal contact with prospective voters, by radio and television or other authorised modern communication means.

There shall be no public election rallies unless they are party conventions held in a suitable house, enclosed space or hall in which the normal daily life of the environment, in which the convention is held, is not disrupted.

Contravention of this rule shall attract a prison sentence for all those party officers and executives convicted.

9. The Security Forces

The security forces of the country shall consist of the army, air force and navy for national defence, the police for internal defence and other branches of these for specialised security services to the country, such as the national guard, civil defence agency, disaster or emergency relief agency, etc.

These forces shall be, as specified in the constitution, under the control of the appropriate and/or elected persons or committees and shall, under no circumstances, seize, control or interfere in political process or power.

To ensure that this is so, all the commands in all the security forces shall be state based with a national command composed of commanders from each of the states. The head of a national command shall be elected by the state commanders and must secure sixty five percent of the valid votes. His or her tenure of office shall be two years with options for renewal up to a total of ten years of service.

Each state command will be autonomous deriving its revenue and support from a constitutionally specified percentage contribution from the state and the federal government.

There shall be only state and national police with clearly defined roles, responsibilities and limits of power and operation. It shall, also, be organised like the armed forces.

10. Remuneration of Elected Public Office Holders

The remuneration of all elected public officers including the President, governors and chairmen of local governments shall be in accordance with a public service pay structure taking into account their relative positions in authority and responsibility *vis a vis* the rest of the civil and public service. In all cases, their salaries and allowances shall be the median salary of comparable groups.

For example, the president's salary shall be comparable to the median salary of chief executives of the largest corporations operating in the country. That of national senators shall be comparable to the median salary of divisional managers of large corporations in the country.

Similarly the salary of state legislators shall be comparable to the median salary of middle managers of large corporations in the country while the salary of local government councillors shall be comparable to the median salary of junior managers of large corporations in the country.

Neither the president nor any of the elected senators, legislators or councillors shall determine their salaries and allowances which shall be in accordance with regular civil and public service structures.

11. Remuneration of Established Public Office Holders

Public and civil servants shall be remunerated according to the existing civil service structure and levels. The actual amounts attached to these grades and levels must, however, be such that the minimum wage cannot be below what is needed to support a single unmarried person with a minimum of the first school leaving certificate in reasonable comfort.

The salary ratio between the lowest paid worker and the highest paid worker in the public service shall not be greater than ten.

12. Conflict of Interest

It shall be a criminal offence for an elected official or public servant to benefit, directly or by proxy, from any legislation or decision in which, as an elected representative of the people or public servant, he is party to. This includes all members of his nuclear and extended family.

All elected officials and public servants and members of his nuclear and extended family, involved in a particular benefit decision, subject to not being found guilty of any criminal offence, shall be rewarded with those items which were ordinarily available to other citizens which, because of their position, they could not vie for.

This shall not apply to every elected or public office holders but only to those who were denied these benefits because of their sensitive position with regard to the particular benefit

13. Government Business and Revenue

No government shall own any natural or artificial resource such as minerals or commercial enterprises except they are research or regulatory agencies, educational institutions, hospitals and homes for the elderly, disabled, etc.

Government shall not appoint any part or aspect of management of, or control directly or indirectly, any commercial enterprise, except its research or regulatory agencies, educational institutions, hospitals and homes for the elderly, disabled, etc and in all cases only as determined by law

All government revenue shall be only in the form of taxes whether income, excise, duties, royalty or any such recognised form of tax.

Income tax exemption shall apply to an amount of income to be determined by the appropriate government in power after which there will be a flat rate tax for income above this level at a rate to be determined by the experts.

There shall be no inheritance tax but all inherited assets or money must present evidence of having paid due taxes during their acquisition.

Excise duties, royalties and sales tax shall never exceed five percent.

The rate of depreciation of company or any assets shall be such that no industry or person shall be allowed to exploit its unique or sensitive position.

There shall be no tax holidays or such inducements for any company new or established.

No company shall declare a gross profit of more than ten percent in any year. Any gross profit in excess of ten percent in any year shall automatically be the property of government and shall be used only to fund its free educational and healthcare services.

Company tax, the rate of which shall be determined by experts in consideration of the above, shall, also, be flat rate without exemptions and inducements.

Because companies and individuals may misrepresent their costs and revenues for the purpose of tax evasion, the APIP shall study, define and monitor at local, state and national levels, the costs and acceptable revenues associated with doing business in the country.

14. Social Services and Welfare

The first priority of the APIP when it gets into government will be to create zones, known in the USA as zip codes and in the UK as post codes.

Each post code or group of post codes shall have at least one nursery school, one primary school, one each of secondary grammar, technical and modern schools and one general hospital.

Each local government or viable group of local governments shall have one polytechnic, university, one university teaching hospital, one water borehole and either a wind or solar electricity generating station as part of the national grid

Education shall be tuition free at all levels but the students will have to pay their living, book and transport expenses.

Admission to schools of choice shall be by academic merit only, determined fairly and rigorously.

Hospital treatment shall be free at all government hospitals.

All chronically sick and elderly people sixty five years of age who do not have a pension shall be entitled to the welfare benefit of the cost of accommodation, if they have no house of their own, and living costs to the minimum necessary to live to a standard commensurate with their education and training in their environment provided that there is authentic evidence that they have been at work previously and paid their taxes. Previously employed but now unemployed persons and new graduates who are unemployed may also be entitled to unemployment befits for a specified length of time.

15. Freedom of Conscience or Religion

All citizens, residents and visitors in the country shall be free, without let or hindrance, to practice their religion or follow their conscience provided that such practices do not prevent others from doing the same thing or their practice is injurious to the health and/or physical safety of the practitioner or others.

Such freedoms do not include the freedom to practice human sacrifice, abortion, mutilation of limbs, in any form or guise, or that of homosexuality, bestiality and all such forms of sexual or other aberrations.

16. Freedom from Discrimination

It is in the nature of human beings to discriminate between good and bad and to avoid things or people that they perceive to be dangerous or harmful to their good health, peace of mind or survival.

What is defined as good or bad in any society is determined by its culture, its history and its accepted religion.

In spite of the diversity of cultures and peoples, there is an amazing agreement among all peoples in this world and in many areas of human endeavour about what is good and what is bad.

Unfortunately, some parts of Western Europe and the Americas have reduced this natural tendency of human beings to discriminate to a hateful, ethnic directed and wicked exercise in which untold cruelty and bestiality have been visited on vulnerable, peaceful and law abiding peoples only because of the colour of their skin, their ethnic origins or inability to defend themselves.

The eventual, though still partial, recognition, in these countries, of the evil nature of these hateful activities, has generated an overreaction in those countries in which, to avoid further discrimination, laws are being passed and enforced such that nothing can be regarded as good or bad anymore.

The consequence is the re-emergence and legalisation in these countries of age old abominable practices whose only end result will be the destruction of civilised society and the end of the human race.

While the African Peoples Independence Party will not execute homosexuals, paedophiles and abortionists, it considers such practices unnatural and inimical to a stable, happy and healthy society. Such practices are not acceptable in an authentic African environment

The African Peoples Independence Party shall, therefore, legislate against open declaration of such practices in such a manner that those found guilty shall be subjected by law to medical or psychological treatment.

Foreigners who visit or are resident in the country must sign the declaration that they shall abide by these laws or shall be refused entry into the country. It will be the policy of the African Peoples Independence Party governments to deport homosexuals and paedophiles at their expense if they are foreigners or visitors who refuse to sign this declaration and to arrest and send them to appropriate centres for medical treatment whether or not they are citizens.

No abortion shall be carried out unless it is to save the life of the mother and by an authorised and certified medical practitioner. Any other abortion, under the African Peoples Independence Party government, shall be considered murder and liable, on conviction, to life imprisonment.

The African Peoples Independence Party shall set up homes for unwed mothers in which they can have and nurse their babies up to six months after birth. With the national DNA database, such homes shall also identify the fathers of these children.

17. Freedom of Speech and Association

The APIP will guarantee freedom of speech and association under the terms and conditions specified in the Constitution and internationally recognised statutes and codes of law which do not condone abortion, homosexuality and such practices.

18. Freedom of Movement and from Harrassment

The practice of road safety task forces, police and military checkpoints, of arrest without charge or notice and of confiscation of property by local, state or national government officials without a court order or as the consequence of a court judgement, will be stopped immediately by the African Peoples Independence Party.

All citizens shall be considered innocent until proven guilty by a competent court of law.

19. Consequences for the Guilty

By guaranteeing these freedoms, the African Peoples Independence Party expects every citizen, resident or visitor in the country, to reciprocate in responsibility, being law abiding, peaceful; and his or her neighbour's keeper.

The African Peoples Independence Party will build enough prisons to take out of circulation, citizens, residents or visitors who seek to make life uncomfortable, unsafe or dangerous for law abiding citizens.

There shall be no capital punishment for any offence but life imprisonment will be life imprisonment and long prison sentences shall ensure that criminals do not continue to mingle with law abiding citizens. Such prisons shall be well equipped for the inmates to live a life of dignity and personal fulfilment, albeit excluded from mainstream society for the number of years they are in prison.

The situation where stealing a fowl attracts a six months prison sentence while robbing the state of millions as a public officer attracts, in some cases, a mild reprimand shall stop. Every punishment shall suit the crime regardless of the status of the offender.

The immunity granted to public officers shall be restricted only to direct relevance to their carrying out their functions and not to their office. A governor, president, chief of police or army staff or general who runs over a child with his or her car shall be prosecuted like anyone else and if convicted, shall be meted the appropriate punishment including being sent to prison.

20. Legal Contracts

All legal contract documents shall be clear and transparent. No clause which can have the effect of changing the nature or terms of a contract shall be in small print

21. Retrenchment of Workers

A popular strategy used by management to maintain profit levels, improve efficiency or cut down losses is to retrench workers. The APIP shall legislate that worker retrenchment shall be the last, not the first, resort. There shall be no worker retrenchment in any profit making organisation until the following conditions are met

a. Top, middle and junior management salaries, benefits and perks have been reduced to the median levels in the industry and the company is still unable to solve its financial problems
b. The gross profit margin of the company has become zero and the company is at less than break even

This does not preclude companies from sacking incompetent workers or workers who exploit this ruling to be unproductive in the company.

22. Land, Sea, River and Air Transportation and Travel

The African Peoples Independence Party shall ensure the full development of land, sea, river and air transportation within the country. It shall cause to be designed and built an interconnecting network of modern all season roads for motor vehicle transportation, modern railway systems, stations and tracks and a rational system of modern airports and facilities for air travel within the country.

All possible canal and ferry transport within the country shall be developed for both domestic and tourist travel.

The APIP shall investigate the possibility of making all public transport by bus or train within cities and townships free, to be funded from tax paid by people in these cities or townships

23. Schools and Education

The African Peoples Independence Party shall ensure the full development of all levels and types of schools and education with emphasis on re-establishing cherished and laudable African values.

The core curriculum in all secondary schools, whether vocational, technical or academic, must be grammar school oriented in which compulsory subjects must be the local language, mathematics, history, geography, local or foreign literature and any other foreign language that is relevant to the economy all of which must be passed to graduate.

All levels of government and the private sector shall be entitled to establish and manage schools at all levels provided that the rules on profit, tax and staff retrenchment for profit oriented enterprises are complied with.

Every local government area must have at least one set of pre-primary, primary, secondary and tertiary educational institution established by the local government, state or private sponsors.

Tuition or the direct teaching cost shall be free in all schools but students must pay for their transport, accommodation, books and supplies.

24. Hospitals

The African Peoples Independence Party shall ensure the full development of hospitals, both public and private, at all local, state and national levels.

All levels of government and the private sector shall be entitled to establish and manage hospitals provided that the rules on profit, tax and staff retrenchment for profit oriented enterprises are complied with.

Every local government area must have at least one full service hospital established by the local or state government or private sponsors.

All hospitals, whether private or public, shall operate the government approved free healthcare system to the standard and extent specified by the law.

25. Housing, Urban and Regional Planning

The African environment and culture are, currently, under threat from Westernised concepts of housing, urban and regional planning. Western ideas of housing, urban and regional planning tend to be artificial, creating postcard picture scenery and environments which are not conducive to regular human habitation and happiness.

It operates by bulldozing and destroying natural environments and habitats and recreating some other picturesque but artificial ones thereby creating more problems which create even more problems as attempts are made to solve the problems they create.

The authentic African concept, however, is based on centuries of experience and harmonious living with nature. There is usually the central market place and place of gathering for feasts or festivities. Several footpaths lead to and from this centre and to other dwellings. Its equivalent in Europe and the Americas, fast disappearing, is what is called DOWN TOWN, INNER CITY, etc.

Then there are safe public storage places where whatever is left there cannot be stolen. Its equivalent in Europe and the Americas is what is called safe lockers found at railway stations and post offices.

The distinguishing feature of African housing, urban and regional planning, however, is the consideration it gives to the family. A typical African family does not just consist of the nuclear family but what Western labelling calls the extended family. This term does not quite capture the full facts of the situation.

A typical African family, in reality, consists of the grandparents, the children and the grandchildren living together, usually in the same compound with the eldest son. Other grown up and married brothers, sisters, and uncles, aunts, nephews, nieces, cousins and in-laws live elsewhere, usually, close by and form, what Western labelling calls, the extended family.

In terms of housing design, a nuclear family's housing unit must accommodate the grandparents as well as the members of the nuclear family. The benefit is that old parents get looked after and the little grandchildren get looked after also by their grandparents while their parents are free to go to work without worrying about who would look after their young children.

This system also helps to entrench the right morality and peace between husband and wife as well as general happiness and fair dealing in the family.

The APIP will, also, legislate that air conditioning shall be a standard feature in all houses and accommodation in cities and townships.

Although the damage has been done by Western influences in most current African cities and townships, most rural communities, south of the Sahara, are still not far from the authentic African model.

It shall be the major objective of the APIP to preserve and modernise these communities along the lines of African culture and seek to reverse the degradation of the cities and townships by prohibiting any future residential development which does not incorporate, in a flat or house for example, accommodation for grandparents and children.

The APIP shall de-emphasise population concentration in cities and shall encourage intelligent and African oriented urban and regional sprawls in which green vegetation and natural footpaths predominate.

There shall be three types of housing in urban areas namely company housing, private and individual housing and retired, disabled and elders housing. Each shall be designed to be in harmony with nature and with the needs of the occupants and can be sponsored by anybody. Rent and tenure shall be as specified by law.

26. Power and Energy

The APIP shall encourage the use of the full mix of power resources available in the country with emphasis on environmental impact and use of renewable resources.

Hydro electricity, voltaic and non-voltaic solar energy,

wind power, fossil fuel and nuclear energy shall be encouraged with power being given to local or regional management of these within a national grid.

The APIP will investigate and seek in a referendum whether and if citizens in the country would like to pay a little more tax to get residential electricity free and at what levels this tax might be.

27. Agriculture and Land Development

It is amazing that Africa south of the Sahara, with the most fertile and arable lands in Africa, suffers from draught or starvation and have to depend on food imports from the Americas, Europe and the Far East.

The APIP will modernise land tenure systems to take land out of the control of governments, speculators and other parasites in the system and restore land ownership and control to previous norms applicable to the region of the country.

If an indigenous land tenure system proves incapable of meeting the demands of a modern African society, the solution is not to scrap it and replace it with Government controlled Western systems which does not work in Africa but to apply indigenous thought and solution.

A look at the current organised food industry in most African countries south of the Sahara shows that they are mostly engaged in the production of European type bread, cakes and buns, tea, soft drinks, malt drinks, beers and spirits, cocoa and chocolate drinks, sweets and toffees, pasta and spaghetti, etc.

There is no country in Africa, south of the Sahara, where any major component of the staple diet consumed by the majority indigenous population is manufactured on a large scale by any major food or beverage manufacturer.

While these companies are feeding Africans with their toxic diet of chemicals and sugar, it is the peasant farmer, with no encouragement from any quarter, who is feeding this indigenous population in these countries.

The APIP will encourage the agricultural production and processing of native indigenous niche or mass consumption crops and will no longer allow the preferential production of tea, cocoa and wheat to displace local products. This does not mean that these products will not be produced but the emphasis must be the production of indigenous foods and products.

28. <u>Water Supply and Management</u>

Another amazing fact about Africa south of the Sahara is that in spite of an abundance of numerous fresh water streams and resources, it suffers from draught and water borne diseases. It shall be a priority of the APIP to deal with this anomaly and organise better management of our abundant water resources.

29. <u>The Manufacturing Industry</u>

The origins of the modern manufacturing industry tend to be obscured by the egocentric propaganda of Europe and the consequent, apparent, irreversibility of hectic modern involvement in it.

Modern manufacturing industry arose from the so called industrial revolution which arose because of hardship, scarcity and desperation in European countries. These conditions had, also, fuelled the search for sources of raw materials which gave rise to the fourteenth to the nineteenth century colonialism and slavery.

The industrial revolution and its aftermath were brutal, cruel and inhuman regimes whose effects are still being felt even today. Modern industry, no matter how much it tries, is still a cruel, inhuman and dangerous activity. It is still a desperate activity with callous retrenchments, disastrous accidents and creeping devaluation of human life.

Africa, south of the Sahara, has, fortunately, no such history. It is suicidal, therefore, for it to try to emulate the industrial philosophy of Europe. All the theories of economy of scale associated with European type manufacturing have now been superseded by more modern concepts such as economy of scope, just-in-time technologies, flexible manufacturing, etc. - new names and garbs for what Africans have been practising for centuries but were laughed at.

The APIP will encourage industrial manufacturing which emphasises small to medium sized industries over large ones. This provides flexibility in product and quantity manufacturing, encourages entrepreneurship and limits business failures to small groups rather than catastrophic deaths of large cities based on the business failure of one large manufacturing plant.

A chemical or food production plant can be of the skid mounted type which can be operated by few personnel and able to be located in a small standard plot occupying not more than 600 square metres. An appliance manufacturing plant, for example for refrigerators, air conditioners, etc, can be a small to medium size unit producing a few ten or hundred units a week or a month and managed and operated by a small group of personnel known to each other on first name basis. As with appliances, so with cars, bicycles, motorcycles, etc.

Such small plants are, also, more suited to the

manufacture of African indigenous food, drink and cosmetic products. There is also nothing to say that manufacturing steel, plastics and fibres in such plants will be uneconomic. Such plants also put a human face to manufacturing and provide much better job satisfaction to the entrepreneur and workers.

30. <u>Commerce</u>

Africa, south of the Sahara, used to be ridiculed in Europe for its so called primitive commerce.

Credit cards, internet and online shopping and so called modern marketing and selling techniques have given the Africans the last laugh and it is only the beginning. All the complex procedures, laws, regulations and court litigations in so called modern business are beginning to show that good old, honest and simple dealing is the best, what Africans were laughed at for doing and considered to be not very smart.

Western nations can, however, be excused because they did not have the freedom to chose as Africans had and still have.

Even though most African countries, south of the Sahara, have become enmeshed in the so called modern commerce, the APIP will impose the African flavour to it by dealing very harshly with dishonest and sharp business practices.

It shall introduce price labelling, issuing of receipts and small change for every commercial transaction, validation of weights and measures, which are welcome components of European business practice. It shall abolish the small print in all contracts and the charging of exorbitant fees for any service. Local governments shall be empowered to determine and fix, in consultation with the professional society involved, the scale and levels of professional fees charged in both the private and public sector within its area of authority. Such scale and level of fees can be challenged in court by any citizen.

31. Banking and Finance

The APIP recognises the important and critical contributions which the banking and finance industry makes in any economy and would continue to sponsor, promote and protect such activities.

Current events in the banking and finance industry show, however, that the industry is disdainful of the trust placed on it by its clients and by government.

In keeping with the avowed objective of the APIP to restore the honest and fair environment that was characteristic of Africa, south of the Sahara, an APIP government would ensure that banking practices would be fair to all and sundry.

In particular, the retail banking arm of the industry would be separated from its investment arm. Banking salaries, wages, commissions, fees and bonuses would be made to be in line with the general principle that the ratio of the totality of the highest pay to the lowest pay shall never exceed ten.

Interest rates, while not losing sight of prevailing market rates must, however, be such that gross profit in the industry does not exceed the national limit of ten percent.

Any bank, which thinks such terms are unattractive, is free to move its businesses to countries which will allow it to exploit their citizens.

As with the banking industry, so with the insurance

and with the independent, non-bank credit industries.

The APIP does not wish to encourage false appearances of business and economic success which traditional activities of the banking and finance industry promote only to result in painful retrenchments and economic cycles of boom and bust.

32. Youths, Sports and Culture

Africa's biggest asset and expertise are in its youth and its culture. Colonial brainwashing and forced structures have tried but are yet to succeed in snuffing out this wealth.

The APIP will prioritise the resuscitation of African drama, storytelling, songs and dancing that enabled African slaves in the Americas and the West Indies to, not only survive the cruelties meted out to them but also, rise like phoenixes to influence and dominate the world popular music scene.

The APIP will resuscitate and encourage indigenous African sports as well as modern Western sporting activities. It will encourage the setting up of sports associations such as football associations, tennis associations, etc and the building of stadia and sports centres by both the government and the private sector.

Western culture tends to associate the approval or disapproval of certain practices with religion. Thus, same sex marriages, teenage pregnancies, single motherhood, promiscuity, abortion and divorce are considered, in Western thinking, to be practices frowned upon or prohibited because of religious principles.

This is contrary to African culture which sees these things in their true perspective as human actions which have painful and undesirable human consequences.

African family and marriage systems, not those imposed by Christianity and Islam and mistaken for the African viewpoint, have been designed and operated for centuries to give equal and fair rights to both men and women.

In authentic African culture, a father cannot impose a husband on his daughter or force her to marry anyone. Her free and independent consent must be obtained. Neither husband nor wife has unchallengeable rights over each other's life. It is not done for an unmarried girl to be pregnant. Even then, there are well established remedies for dealing with it if the father is known or if the father is unknown or unacceptable.

Love, in the Western sense, is considered an infatuation (as proven by the frequency of divorce). In the African system, there is an elaborate and prolonged process, verified and witnessed at every stage by friends and relatives in the marriage process so that when the marriage is eventually formalised, everybody knows what is expected of him or her and what he or she will expect to get out of the marriage.

Even when the marriage hits the rocks, there is an elaborate system of checks and balances and avenues for complaint and redress that, overall, a married couple is usually very happy, secure and satisfied with each other, warts and all.

The current problem in African countries, south of the Sahara, is that only the ceremonial elements of the authentic African culture are been incorporated into the hedonistic components of Western culture, ignoring the responsibility and authenticity components in both cultures.

Current Western driven African culture is typified by mindless selfishness, envy and ganging up against perceived enemies or people doing better than one. For pecuniary and other benefits, the modern African may sell his mother or brother without batting an eyelid. It is easy to blame this on survival instinct needed to survive the impositions of Western colonialism. It is, also, not that Africans were saints before colonialism because one has to be a kind of character to react to certain stimulus in a certain way. The real culprit is the abandonment of authentic African training.

The APIP will set out to correct this situation by enacting legislation which, without interfering with the religious or other sensibilities of the participants, ensures that broken families, promiscuity, abortion, etc, are limited. One of such measures is the introduction of the DNA database for births, marriages and deaths. The other is the introduction of homes where unmarried pregnant women can live and deliver their babies at state expense for up to six months after birth. Another is the specification that all homes must include accommodation for grandparents. There will be many more introduced as the government of the APIP settles down.

33. Foreign Policy

Most African governments, south of the Sahara, are in the iron grips of their former colonial masters or other Western and Eastern countries and Powers. They find themselves as pawns in the macabre game of Western power politics whose basic aim is to destabilise and keep in perennial instability any power or country not their own. By so doing, they expect to be continually relevant as peace makers, rebuilders of the economy or as charitable friends in times of need.

Any leader of a country which refuses to play this game is vilified, badmouthed, libelled and sanctioned to submission or overthrown by gullible citizens of those countries. Usually, these overthrown leaders were, previously, gullible persons who the Western countries used to overthrow a previous leader.

The government of the APIP will not be an isolated government in world and regional affairs. The APIP government will be friends and neighbours to all countries but its major preoccupation shall be the welfare and security of its citizens. Its system of political organisation will be such that there will be no permanent or very powerful leaders. Since the country is formed by people who chose to live with each other in one country, the standard trick of Western powers to divide and rule will be less effective.

34. Domestic Policy

The details of domestic policy have been spelt out in the various sections of this manifesto. The overall philosophy however, is that every citizen of the country governed by APIP has equal rights, privileges and responsibilities as any other citizen.

Every citizen is entitled to equal protection and security of care, of education, of employment, of healthcare, of housing, of transportation and of every other benefit that is reasonable to expect from one's country. That includes those who are disabled or physically challenged, unemployed or elderly. All these are to be done within an authentic African social and cultural framework

The rationale for promoting the system of short term and not overly powerful leaders and legislators is to ensure that real power belongs to the people. Leaders and legislators do not need to learn on the job because when they chose to contest the seat, they had offered to give their expertise, acquired in their chosen fields, for the benefit of the nation. In any case, they will be, and are, supported by experienced civil servants.

Their job will be to bring in their rich and direct experience as well as an overview of what the average citizen is experiencing and propose solutions. If their experience, in their working life, does not give them sufficient knowledge of what the country needs, then they are failures and should be voted out in two, four or six years and if they manage to have succeeded in deceiving the electorate to stay a second term, they cannot come back for a third.

If they are so good that they could be good for a third term, it is derogatory to their constituency that it has only one person good enough to represent them.

www.ingramcontent.com/pod-product-compliance
Lightning Source LLC
Chambersburg PA
CBHW022132280326
41933CB00007B/658